LearnEnglish
WithAfrica

The Perfect Present, with the Present Perfect

LEVEL B1-B2

Reading Comprehension and
Grammar Worksheets

By
Thandi Ngwira Gatignol

CONTENTS

FOREWORD

There are many advantages to reading short stories when you are learning English.

First of all, short stories are 'short', therefore you a get a sense of accomplishment much quicker than when you read a novel.

Secondly, you encounter different interesting characters and you can put yourself in their shoes. This can be done by appropriating the way they think or talk. Vocabulary is thus easier to grasp and digest.

Thirdly, language and grammatical structures are seen in context. Hence, you will gain a deeper understanding of how words, tenses and punctuation work together to form meaning.

Finally, reading short stories gives you access to valuable cultural information about a people, country or continent.

I hope that *The Perfect Present, with The Present Perfect* meets your expectations and fosters your own creativity.

Thandi Ngwira Gatignol, Founder (Learn English With Africa)

SHORT STORY

The Perfect Present

Have you ever given somebody a present and they destroyed it right in front of your eyes? Well, believe it or not, this happened to me three days ago. My husband tore his Valentine's day gift and my heart hasn't stopped beating wildly since then.

It's the first time I have seen such a reaction from him. I have known Christopher since primary school. For some reason, we only became a couple when we met here again eleven years ago. We have been married for almost a decade now. During that entire period, he has never done anything as surprising as what he did on the 14th of February.

People can change, I realise. People can change, and you can't see that they are changing until it's too late.

There is nothing that could have prepared me for this. Until three days ago, he was still the same kind and generous spirit I have loved and cherished all these years.

We don't have any children yet but we have been talking about having some in the near future. Being abroad is not easy, you know, when it comes to getting stable and respectable jobs that can enable you to raise your kids in a dignified way. I know that this issue has been weighing heavily on him.

Let me tell you one thing. Christopher is one of the brightest people I know. He is smart and given the right opportunities he can go very far in life. His parents have always told him this. When we were at school, our teachers often impressed on him that he would become a doctor that could heal many people in our country.

After he started working, his diligence did not escape his employers' notice either. He was given more responsibilities of course without a corresponding hike in his salary. Christopher did not complain at the time because he was grateful for simply having a job. It never crossed his mind that he could be more demanding.

Recently, it has dawned upon him though that he might never be able to house his family properly on such a meagre income. He has seen his colleagues with similar qualifications getting promotions and buying houses in pretty neighbourhoods and he knows that this kind of life is out of reach for him. We currently live in a dingy one-bedroomed house and we cannot afford to have an extra room, even on our two salaries.

I have never known Christopher to be a bitter or resentful person. You know, life has not been really kind to him compared to what his peers have been through at the same age, yet, you will never hear him complaining. Never. He wakes up very early in the morning. He does whatever he has to do. After he knocks off from work, he comes back home and helps me with the housework even when I can tell that he is about to fall from physical and emotional exhaustion.

This is why I thought that the present was such a great idea!

Dear friends, I have come to a point in life where I don't believe in this 'immigration miracle' anymore. You know, we left our homes because the grass seemed greener here. We were disillusioned by our leaders whose greedy bellies left nothing for us in terms of health and education infrastructure. Frankly speaking, in the past fourteen years I have been here, life has been far from being rosy. All I can remember is work, hard work, strenuous work, and more work. There is no moment in my life when I do not think of a way that will keep me two steps away from the street.

Paradoxically, the harder you exert yourself, the less you get. Your efforts are not rewarded but you know that you have to keep going because this is the only thing that you can do.

I have met fellow immigrants who have lived here for more than twenty years and they still feel like they are sidelined in so many ways. Some of them have been sitting on the benches of life for so long that they have got so used to it; they don't even think of training themselves anymore. What will it amount to? They ask themselves. What is the purpose of learning new things when none of it will get duly noticed or rewarded?

Don't even talk about having children, they warn us. The children know that they are second-class citizens the moment they step out of the door. Is it wise then to bring them into such an unfriendly environment? Children need love and material things are not enough to make them feel like they are human beings with proper needs and aspirations, they say.

To say the truth, I know that there is no real future for us here. However, I am not the kind of person that will sit down and just watch while many positive things can be done to solve problems. I also know when enough is enough nevertheless.

Hence, there was no hesitation when I took our savings to buy our two one-way tickets to go back home. This was exactly one week ago.

You cannot imagine how happy I felt when I got those precious tickets. I knew that our woes were finally over. I pictured myself eating authentic mangoes and sweet potatoes and not worrying about being assaulted at the supermarket. I saw myself laughing and crying with my family without an ounce of discomfort and fear. I saw my future children playing with their friends in the yard and coming back inside for lunch, chatting about their awesome day and not telling me about bullying. I felt free and I couldn't wait to share this news to my husband.

I presented his air-ticket in wrapping paper for presents and waited for the right time to give it to him.

Up to now, I still can't believe his reaction.

He was surprised when he saw the pretty package of course. He asked me if it was money or a shopping voucher. I told him that he would soon find out. He took a knife and slit the package open.

"Air tickets!" he exclaimed. "Two air tickets back home!" he shouted after a few seconds. "One-way tickets…"

He did not finish his sentence but looked at me instead. If looks could kill, I'm sure I'd have been long dead by now.

"The present is perfect Hannah."

I stared at him. I thought this was what he'd always wanted all his life!

"Hannah, the present is perfect. We should forget the past and move on. A better future is yet to come. Our life is here now and we have to make the most of it. Everything will be alright, you'll see. The good deeds a man has done before defend him. We will make it no matter what it takes. We have to keep on working hard. The rewards will come in their time. They will, don't worry."

Well, you know, the rest is history...

He tore the air tickets and told me to forget about everything. How can I? There comes a time when feeding on hope and lies is no longer enough. You need something concrete to keep you going.

Forgetting is an impossible task.

Thinking that the situation will get better on its on is an impossible task.

I cannot forget.

I guess the damage has been done.

It is difficult to come back to the present and face reality when all I have been doing the past days is to dream about what I will do once I reach home and see my family.

I long for home.

I long for normalcy.

I long for a place where I will simply be.

Yet, I see Christopher and his optimism. He believes that everything will be alright in the end. Oh Christopher, my very optimistic Christopher.

Every day he reminds me that it is dangerous to live in the past. He says that if you aren't too careful, the past can drag you back and keep you from moving forward.

The past is a dangerous place to permanently live in, he insists. Move on Hannah. Move on.

Christopher avoids any talk that does not help him advance in life. Daily complaints never helped anyone in this world, he says. Save your energy for constructive things, Hannah. This world is not fair. Accept this fact and try to whatever small thing you can do to correct the situation. Complaining will lead us nowhere.

What has he been doing all this time?

He still wakes up very early in the morning to do his everyday tasks.

He hasn't stopped talking about having children here and getting them a decent place to live.

He hasn't backtracked on getting a new job that will finally enable us to move to a better place.

He keeps on urging me to be the best version of myself. He tells me: " Smile to yourself when no one will. Laugh with yourself when no one will. Believe in whatever you are doing when no one will. Being able to do what you are doing is the reward. Do not let negativity affect you in any way. And most of all... don't look back, keep moving and do your best every single day. The present is perfect Hannah, the present is perfect."

THE END

THE PRESENT PERFECT

AFFIRMATIVE FORM (FULL AND SHORT FORMS)							
I	You	He	She	It	We	You	They
have tried	have tried	has tried			have tried		
've tried	've tried	's tried			've tried		

NEGATIVE FORM (FULL AND SHORT FORMS)							
I	You	He	She	It	We	You	They
have not tried	have not tried	has not tried			have not tried		
haven't tried	haven't tried	hasn't tried			haven't tried		

INTERROGATIVE FORM							
Have	Have	Has			Have		
I	you	he	she	it	we	you	they
tried...?							

IRREGULAR VERBS (PART ONE)

VERB STEM	SIMPLE PAST	SIMPLE PRESENT	PRESENT PERFECT
BE	was/were	am/is/are	have/has been
BECOME	became	become/becomes	have/has become
BEGIN	began	begin/begins	have/has begun
BITE	bit	bite/bites	have/has bitten
BREAK	broke	break/breaks	have/has broken
BRING	brought	bring/brings	have/has brought
BUILD	built	build/builds	have/has built
BUY	bought	buy/buys	have/has bought
CHOOSE	chose	choose/chooses	have/has chosen
CUT	cut	cut/cuts	have/has cut
DO	did	do/does	have/has done
DRAW	drew	draw/draws	have/has drawn
DREAM	dreamt	dream/dreams	have/has dreamt
DRINK	drank	drink/drinks	have/has drunk
DRIVE	drove	drive/drives	have/has driven
EAT	ate	eat/eats	have/has eaten
FALL	fell	fall/falls	have/has fallen
FEED	fed	feed/feeds	have/has fed
FEEL	felt	feel/feels	have/has felt
FIGHT	fought	fight/fights	have/has fought
FIND	found	find/finds	have/has found
FLY	flew	fly/flies	have/has flown
GET	got	get/gets	have/has got
GIVE	gave	give/gives	have/has given
GO	went	go/goes	have/has gone
GROW	grew	grow/grows	have/has grown
HAVE	had	have/has	have/has had
HEAR	heard	hear/hears	have/has heard
HIDE	hid	hide/hides	have/has hidden
HIT	hit	hit/hits	have/has hit
KEEP	kept	keep/keeps	have/has kept
KNOW	knew	know/knows	have/has known

IRREGULAR VERBS (PART TWO)

VERB STEM	SIMPLE PAST	SIMPLE PRESENT	PRESENT PERFECT
LAY	laid	lay/lays	have/has laid
LEARN	learnt	learn/learns	have/has learnt
LEAVE	left	leave/leaves	have/has left
LEND	lent	lend/lends	have/has lent
LIE	lay	lie/lies	have/has lain
LOSE	lost	lose/loses	have/has lost
MAKE	made	make/makes	have/has made
MEAN	meant	mean/means	have/has meant
MEET	met	meet/meets	have/has met
PUT	put	put/puts	have/has put
READ	read	read/reads	have/has read
RIDE	rode	ride/rides	have/has ridden
RING	rang	ring/rings	have/has rung
RISE	rose	rise/rises	have/has risen
RUN	ran	run/runs	have/has run
SAY	said	say/says	have/has said
SEE	saw	see/sees	have/has seen
SELL	sold	sell/sells	have/has sold
SEND	sent	send/sends	have/has sent
SHAKE	shook	shake/shakes	have/has shaken
SLEEP	slept	sleep/sleeps	have/has slept
SPEAK	spoke	speak/speaks	have/has spoken
STAND	stood	stand/stands	have/has stood
STEAL	stole	steal/steals	have/has stolen
TAKE	took	take/takes	have/has taken
TEACH	taught	teach/teaches	have/has taught
TELL	told	tell/tells	have/has told
THINK	thought	think/thinks	have/has thought
THROW	threw	throw/throws	have/has thrown
WEAR	wore	wear/wears	have/has worn
WIN	won	win/wins	have/has won
WRITE	wrote	write/writes	have/has written

GRAMMAR WORKSHEETS

1. **PRESENT PERFECT (AFFIRMATIVE FORM):** Find 4 sentences in the short story with the Affirmative form of the Present Perfect.

   E.g.: It's the first time I <u>have seen</u> such a reaction from him.

   a. ....

   ....

   b. ....

   ....

   c. ....

   ....

   d. ....

   ....

2. **PRESENT PERFECT (NEGATIVE FORM):** Find 3 sentences in the short story with the Negative form of the Present Perfect.

   E.g.: I <u>have never known</u> Christopher to be a bitter or resentful person.

   a. ....

   ....

   b. ....

   ....

   c. ....

   ....

3. **<u>PRESENT PERFECT (WRITING)</u>: Make 4 sentences with the Affirmative form of the Present Perfect.**

E.g.: Hannah <u>has lived</u> in Europe for more than ten years.

a. . . . .

. . . .

b. . . . .

. . . .

c. . . . .

. . . .

d. . . . .

. . . .

. . . .

4. **<u>PRESENT PERFECT (WRITING)</u>: Make 4 sentences with the Negative form of the Present Perfect.**

E.g.: They <u>have not gone</u> back home since they arrived more than ten years ago.

a. . . . .

. . . .

b. . . . .

. . . .

c. . . . .

. . . .

d. . . . .

. . . .

. . . .

E.g.: Hannah <u>has lived</u> in Europe for more than ten years.

5. <u>**PRESENT PERFECT (WRITING)**</u>**: Make 4 sentences with the Interrogative form of the Present Perfect.**

E.g.: <u>Have</u> you <u>ever given</u> somebody a present and they destroyed it right in front of your eyes?

a. ....

....

....

b. ....

....

c. ....

....

d. ....

....

....

6. <u>**PRESENT PERFECT and SINCE**</u>**: Make 4 sentences using SINCE.**

E.g.: We have done this <u>since</u> time immemorial.

a. ....

....

b. ....

....

c. ....

....

d. ....

....

....

7. <u>PRESENT PERFECT and FOR</u>: Make 4 sentences using FOR.

E.g.: I have taken this medicine <u>for</u> five days.

a. ....

....

....

b. ....

....

c. ....

....

d. ....

....

....

8. <u>SIMPLE PAST and AGO</u>: Make 4 sentences using AGO and the Simple Past form.

E.g.: She left her country of birth twenty years ago.

a. ....

....

....

b. ....

....

c. ....

....

d. ....

....

....

GENERAL COMPREHENSION

1. <u>GENERAL COMPREHENSION</u>: **Read the short story once again and answer the questions below.**

a. What is the title of the short story?: . . . .
. . . .
. . . .

b. What is the story about?: . . . .
. . . .
. . . .

c. Imagine another title for the short story: . . . .
. . . .
. . . .

d. Who is the narrator?: . . . .

e. How old can he or she be?: . . . .

f. How can you describe the narrator in a few words?: . .
. . . .
. . . .

g. Where does the story take place?: . . . .

h. What are the other places that are mentioned in the story?: . . . .
. . . .
. . . .

i. Pick out another major character in the short story and describe him or her.: . . . .
. . . .
. . . .

DETAILED COMPREHENSION

2. <u>DETAILED COMPREHENSION</u>: **Read the short story once again, paying closer attention to how it was written, and answer the questions below.**
TRUE OR FALSE: Say if the following sentences are TRUE or FALSE. Justify your answer.

a. The narrator is satisfied with living abroad.:. . . . .
. . . .
. . . .

b. Christopher loves Hannah's present.: . . . .
. . . .
. . . .

c. Hannah does not want to be an immigrant forever.: . .
. . . .
. . . .

d. Christopher thinks that his situation will change for the better:. . . . .
. . . .
. . . .

e. Hannah paints a rosy picture of her past: . . . .
. . . .
. . . .

f. Christopher is very pessimistic: . . . .
. . . .
. . . .
. . . .

a. Why did Hannah decide to buy Christopher a present?: . . . .
. . . .
. . . .
. . . .

b. How long has the couple been married?: . . . .
. . . .
. . . .
. . . .

c. Where does the couple live? Are they satisfied with their living conditions?:. . . . .
. . . .
. . . .
. . . .

d. Why does the couple have no children yet?. . . . .
. . . .
. . . .
. . . .

e. How is Christopher viewed by the people around him in general?:. . . . .
. . . .
. . . .
. . . .

f. What is Christopher's attitude towards work? . . . .
. . . .
. . . .
. . . .

g. What reasons does the narrator give to justify the couple's presence abroad? . . . .
. . . .
. . . .
. . . .
. . . .

h. What is Hanna's attitude towards the past?: . . . .
. . . .
. . . .
. . . .
. . . .

i. How does Christopher react to Hannah's present? . .
. . . .
. . . .
. . . .
. . . .

j. Do you think that Christopher should have reacted differently? Justify your answer.: . . . .
. . . .
. . . .
. . . .

k. How does Christopher behave after Valentine's Day?:
. . . .
. . . .
. . . .
. . . .

l. What is Christopher's final advice to Hannah?: . . . . . .
. . . .
. . . .
. . . .
. . . .

WRITTEN EXPRESSION

3. <u>REWRITE THE STORY</u>: Read the short story again and rewrite it from Christopher's point of view. **PAY ATTENTION TO THE FOLLOWING POINTS:**

a. **Plot or Structure:** Think about how your story unfolds and develops in time. What will be the…...?:

Exposition:. . . . .

Rising action:. . . . .

Climax:. . . . .

Falling action: . . . .

Resolution:. . . . .

b. **Vocabulary:** Avoid repeating words unless it is a deliberate, stylistic device. Use descriptive language and show instead of telling.

c. **Grammar:** Pay attention to how you write. Think about tenses, syntax, spelling and punctuation.

d. **Originality:** Make your story as interesting as possible. It should be worth the read.

WRITTEN EXPRESSION CHECKLIST	
My story has a title.	✓
My story has a plot.	✓
I have varied the vocabulary.	✓
I have paid attention to grammar (tenses, syntax, spelling and punctuation.)	✓
My story is original and interesting.	✓

NOTES

www.ingramcontent.com/pod-product-compliance
Lightning Source LLC
LaVergne TN
LVHW041445170726
843492LV00008B/2825